Rub-a-dub-dub

Rub-a-dub-dub,
Three men in a tub,
And who do you think they were?
The butcher, the baker, the candlestick maker;
They all jumped out of a rotten potato;
'Twas enough to make a man stare!

Activity 1

What is technology?

Do you have fun playing with water?
Do you have lots of ideas and invent things?
Technology is all about inventing things.
Inventors need ideas.
Ideas come when you are:

in the bath

in bed

at your desk

when you are day dreaming

What inventions can you see?
Do you wonder why things look as they do?

Collect

favourite water inventions

Look at each one.

★ Why is it needed?
★ Why was it invented?

All of these inventions are technology.
Technology is about helping people and solving problems.

2

The three inventors

The butcher, the baker and the candlestick maker are all inventors.

Why are they in the tub?

They are trying out their water invention.

Make their tub. Make sure their heads are as far away from the water as possible.

You will need

water tray   plastic bottles   plastic bags

elastic bands

plastic container

The plastic bottles can be the butcher, the baker and the candlestick maker.

Say what you think the problem is.

How many different ways can you make your tub?

Which way seems best?

Does it work?

Why does it work or not work?

Be careful ⚠

when blowing up the bags.

Activity 3

Finding out

Was their tub a good invention?

Why do you think they used plastic bags?
Did you put air into your bags?
Can you think of other water inventions which use air as a cushion?

Arm bands, life belts and dinghies use air.
What happens to a dinghy if you don't blow it up?

You will need

arm bands

Blow some arm bands up.
Feel how much force you
can put on it.
When does its shape start
to change?

Why do you think it
becomes so strong when
you put air in it?

Inventing

The three inventors became very interested in air and water. They were very inquisitive.

They decided to make a sail boat.
Help the inventors make a sail which will move the boat across the pool as quickly as possible.

You will need

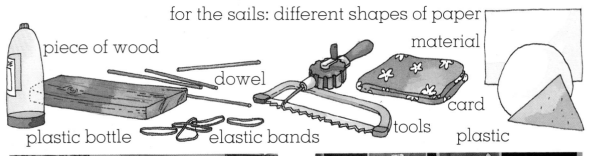

for the sails: different shapes of paper
piece of wood
material
dowel
card
plastic bottle   elastic bands   tools   plastic

First of all make the boat.

Think about the problem of the sails.

Have some ideas. Try a few out.
Make a chart showing what happened.
How will you test the sails?
Make sure your tests are fair.

Fix the best sail to your boat.
How well does it work?

Finding out about sails

Did you find out which sail was best?

* Why was it best?
* Why did it move the boat along?
* How does it work?
* What are the good points of sails?
* What are the bad points?

Sails have been used for hundreds of years.
Sails use the power of moving air to make boats move.
It doesn't cost money for the energy to make them go.

Collect

pictures and books about old sailing boats

Make a big class picture of a sailing boat for your walls.
What else makes the boat move?

Motor boats

Have you ever been in a sailing boat or a motor boat?
Did you like it? Which did you like best?

The butcher, the baker and the candlestick maker wanted to invent a motor boat.
They used a propeller and an electric motor.

You will need

a few different propellers

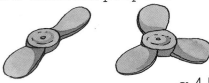

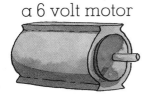
a 6 volt motor

wires

a 4.5 volt battery

First you need to make an electric circuit.
Mary, Mary showed you how to make an
electric circuit.

Be careful

Instead of a light bulb put a motor into the circuit.

★ Can you make the motor work?
★ Where is it getting its energy from?

Activity 7

Fixing the propellers

Have you seen any propellers on boats or other machines?

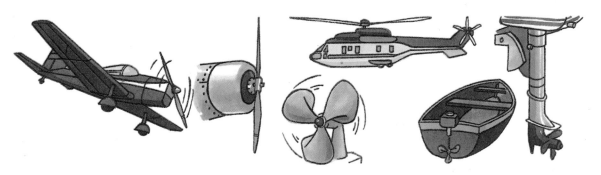

Find out more about how propellers work.
Attach the propeller to the motor.
Make the blades turn around using electricity.

Try different propellers.

Put a switch in.

Polly put the kettle on tells you more about switches.

8

Making the propeller work

The inventors need help to make their boat work with a propeller.

Where on the boat are you going to put the propeller?

Here are some ways of holding propellers. Which do you think will work?

First think about the problem. Tell everyone what you think the problem is.

★ How do you want the boat to move?

★ Where does it need to move to?

1 At the back using elastic bands.

2 High up at the back using plasticine.

3 At the side.

Make a chart showing what happened.

Make your best idea.
Test it.
Tell everyone why you made it like you did and how it works.
Would you change anything?

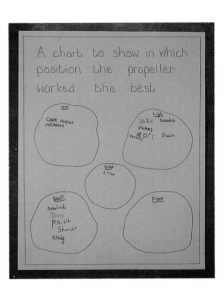

Activity 9

The butcher, the baker and the candlestick maker

Can you put the three inventors into the boat?

You will need  plasticine

Make models of the three inventors out of plasticine.

Find out:

★ how long it takes the boat to move without the men.
★ how long it takes the boat with one, then two, then three men.
★ how many men you need before it won't move at all.

Make a chart of your results. Why do you think there isn't enough energy to make the boat move?

Be an inquisitive technologist.

Help! We are sinking!

Our inventors can't swim.
Help! The boat has capsized!
Will they sink?

Have you wondered why
some things sink?
Do you think things need
energy to sink?

Invent some sinkers out of different materials.
Do some materials sink quickly? Do some materials not sink
at all?
Think about that problem.

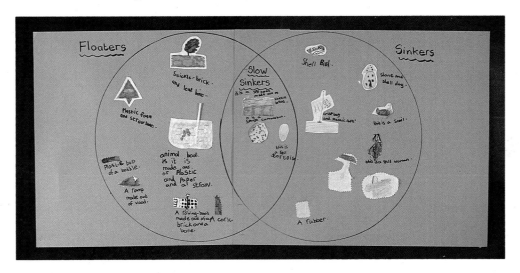

Now invent some things to
stop the inventors sinking.

This big ship can make
people and their suitcases
float!
Isn't that odd?

Activity 11

A new boat

The inventors now want to invent another type of boat for the seaside.

There isn't any wind.
There isn't any electricity left.
Can you think what type of boat you can help them make which has the energy to move?

What do you think people would like at the seaside?
How could you find out what people might like?

Ideas! Ideas! Ideas!

Paint and make a display of your best ideas for a seaside boat.
Write a few sentences about your idea.
Get ready to make it.

Make it.
Test it.
Would children like it?

Let's use elastic

The butcher, the baker and the candlestick maker found elastic!

Feel how stretchy it is.
Give it some energy. Pull it back.
Release it.
Where does it get its energy from?

What kind of things do we use elastic for?
Find other things which are elastic.
What makes something elastic?

The inventors thought elastic was a wonderful invention.
Even when there wasn't any wind or any electricity, they could use elasticity!

Experiment with making an elastic motor to power your boat along.

You will need

wood   your boat

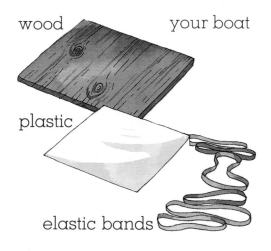

plastic

elastic bands

Activity 13

Improve it!

Did your elastic motor work?

Can you make it go backwards? And forwards! And slow! And fast!!

Tell everyone how it works. Do a drawing of your elastic motor boat and label the parts.

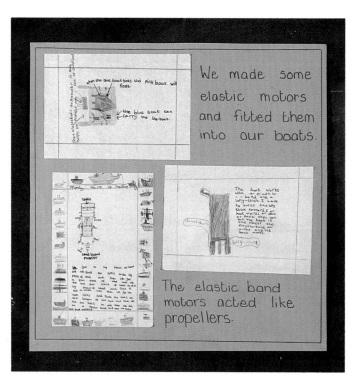

Test it!

Look at how the rest of your class solved the problem.

★ How many different solutions are there?
★ Why do some work better than others?

Talk as a class about it.

Draw a picture of your solution.

Tell the class what you liked about your design.
What would you change?

Activity 15

The technology think-tank

Do you know what a think-tank is ?

The butcher, the baker, the candlestick maker became the think-tank for inventions.

They were the technology think-tank.

Where do you think they held their meetings?
In their tub of course!

Draw a picture of them in their think tank.
Write out the rhyme Rub-a-dub-dub.

What do you think they should invent next?
What is their new problem?